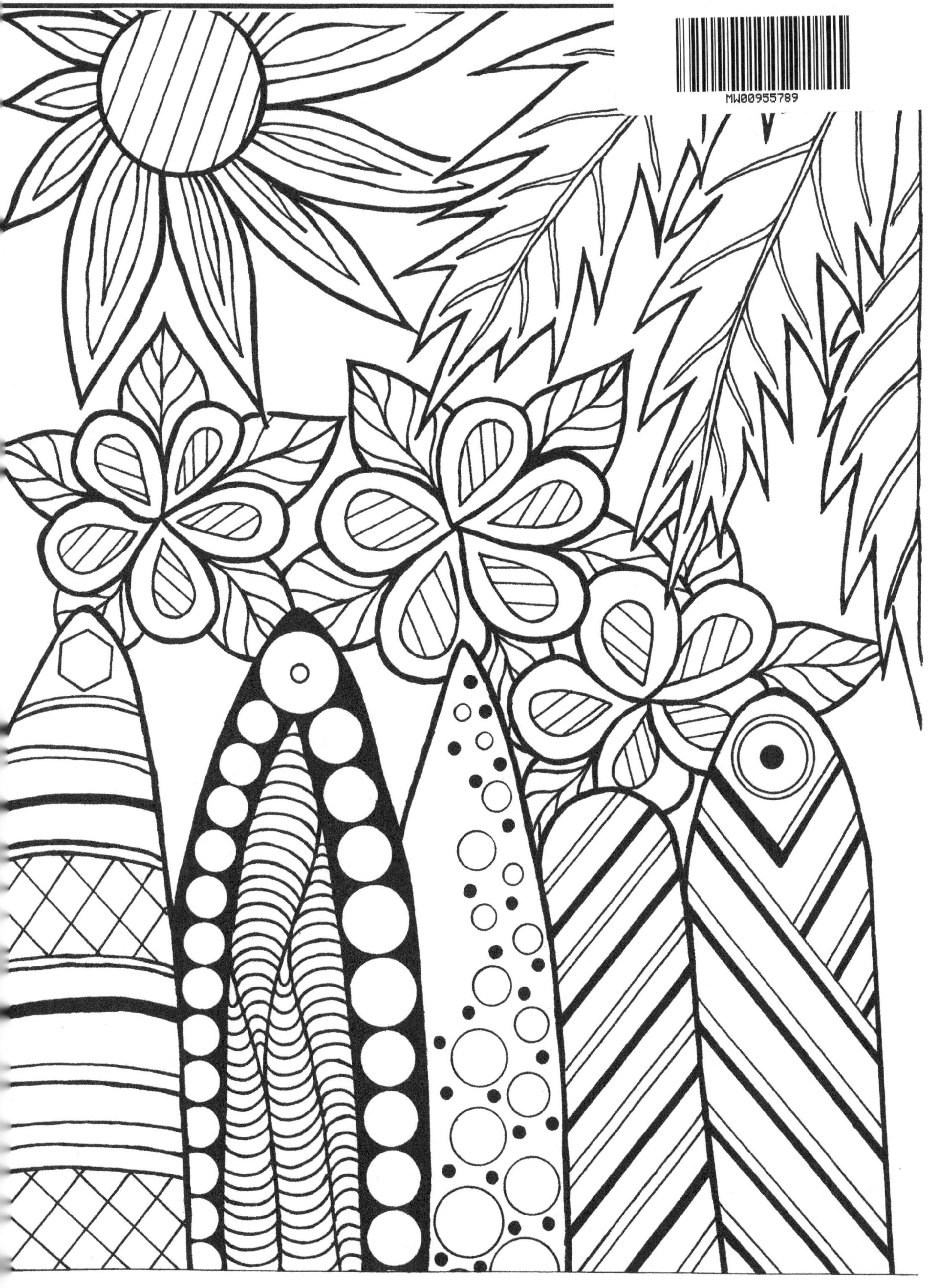

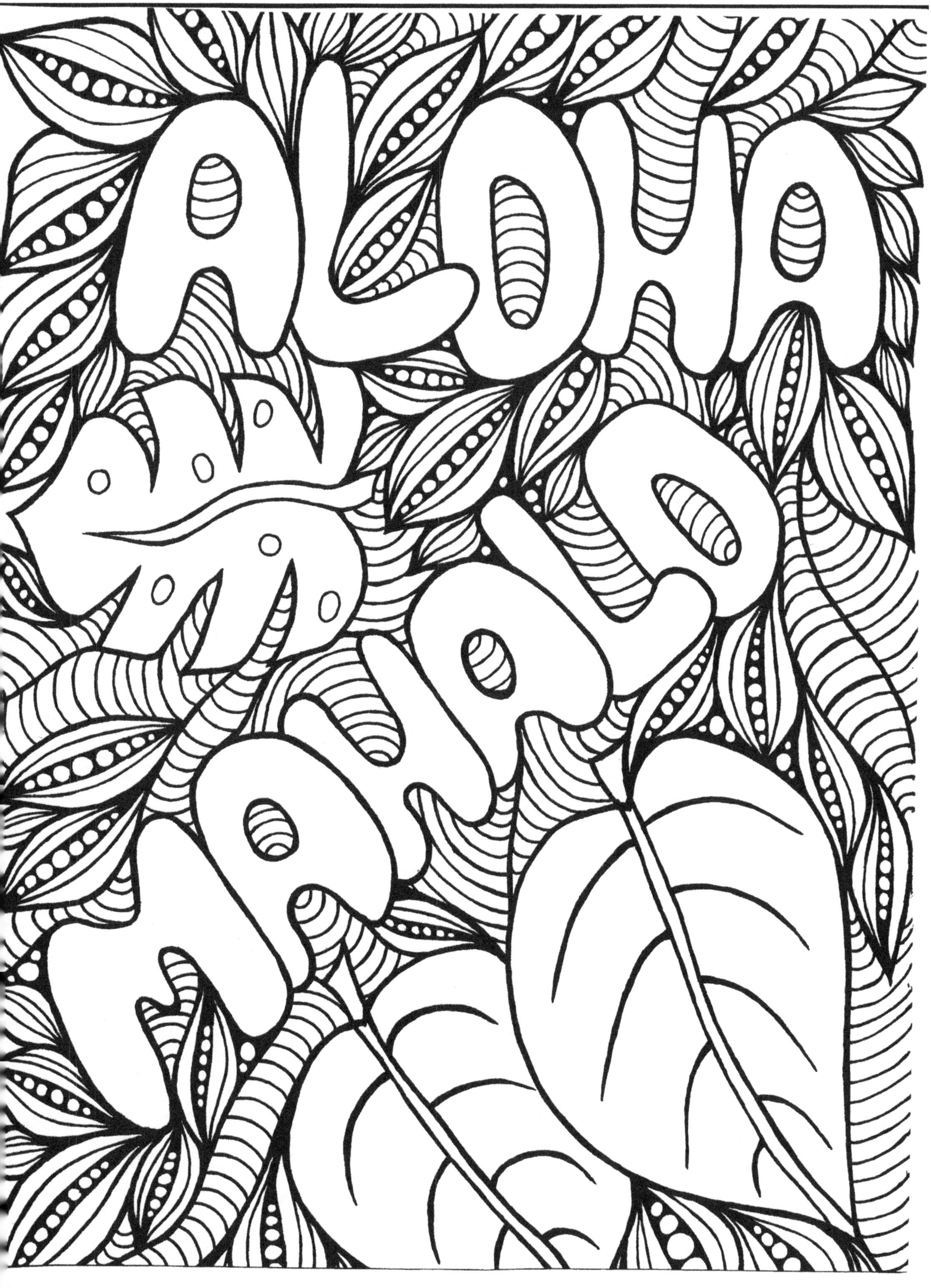
ALOHA
MAHALO

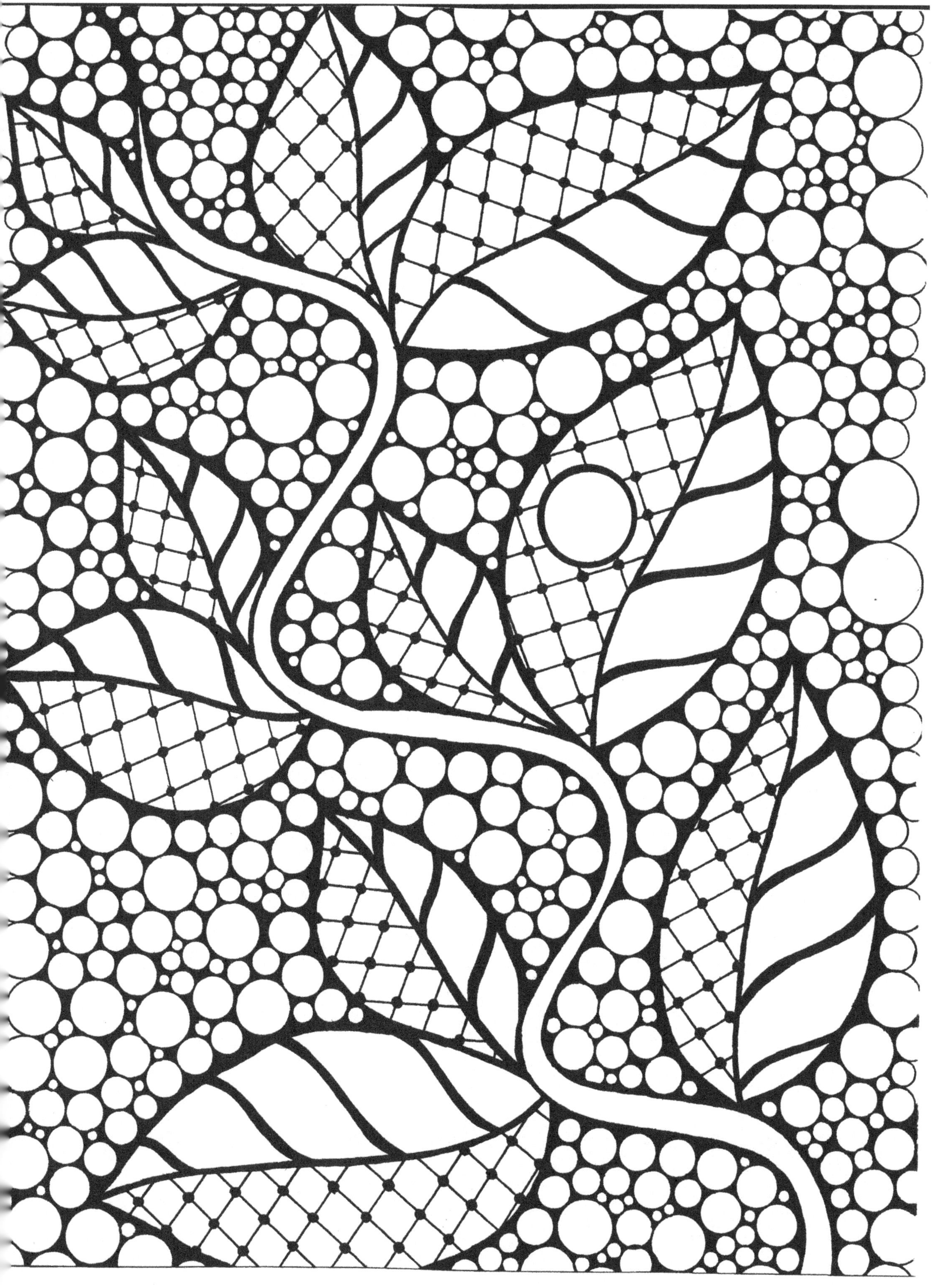

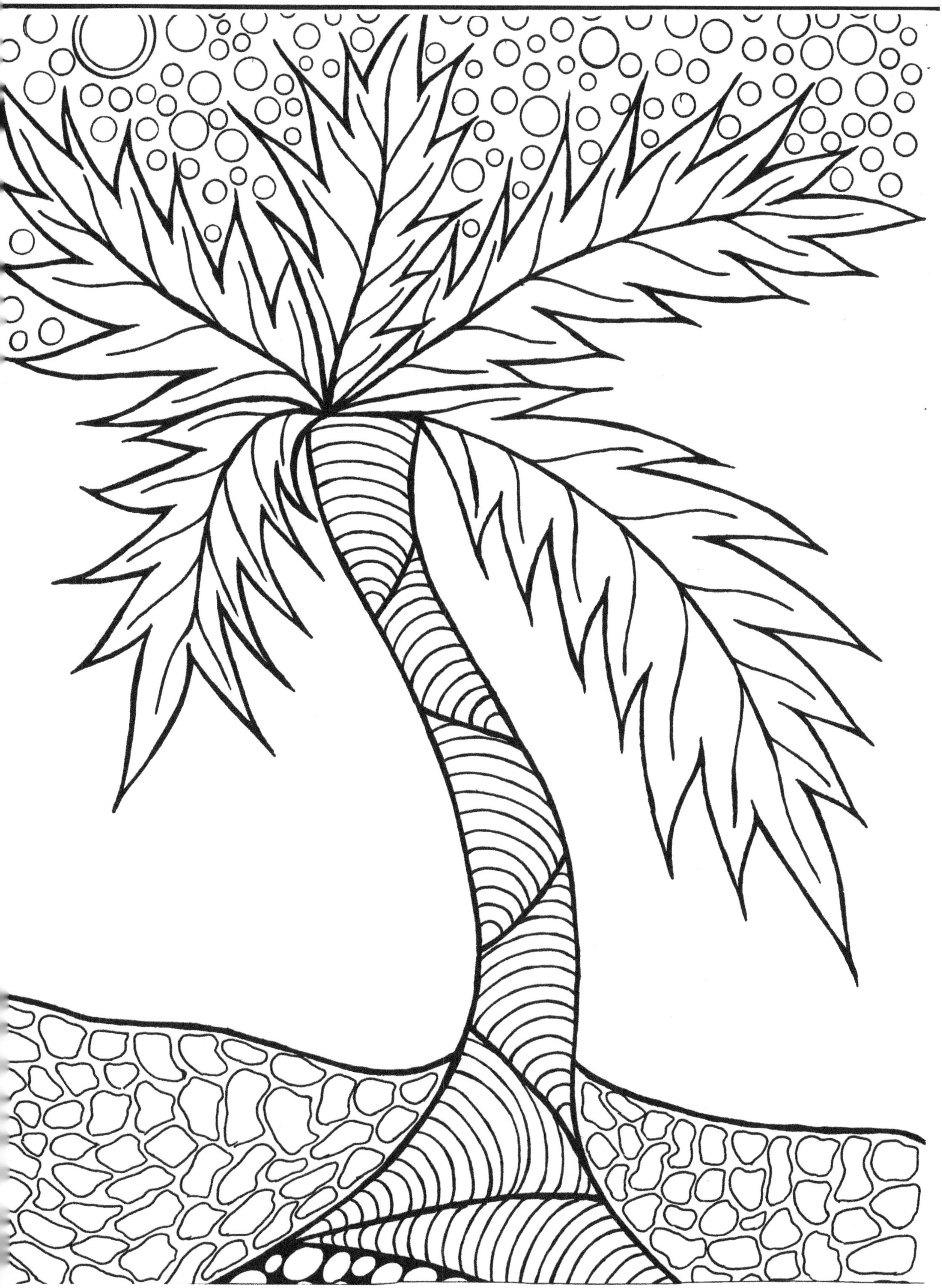

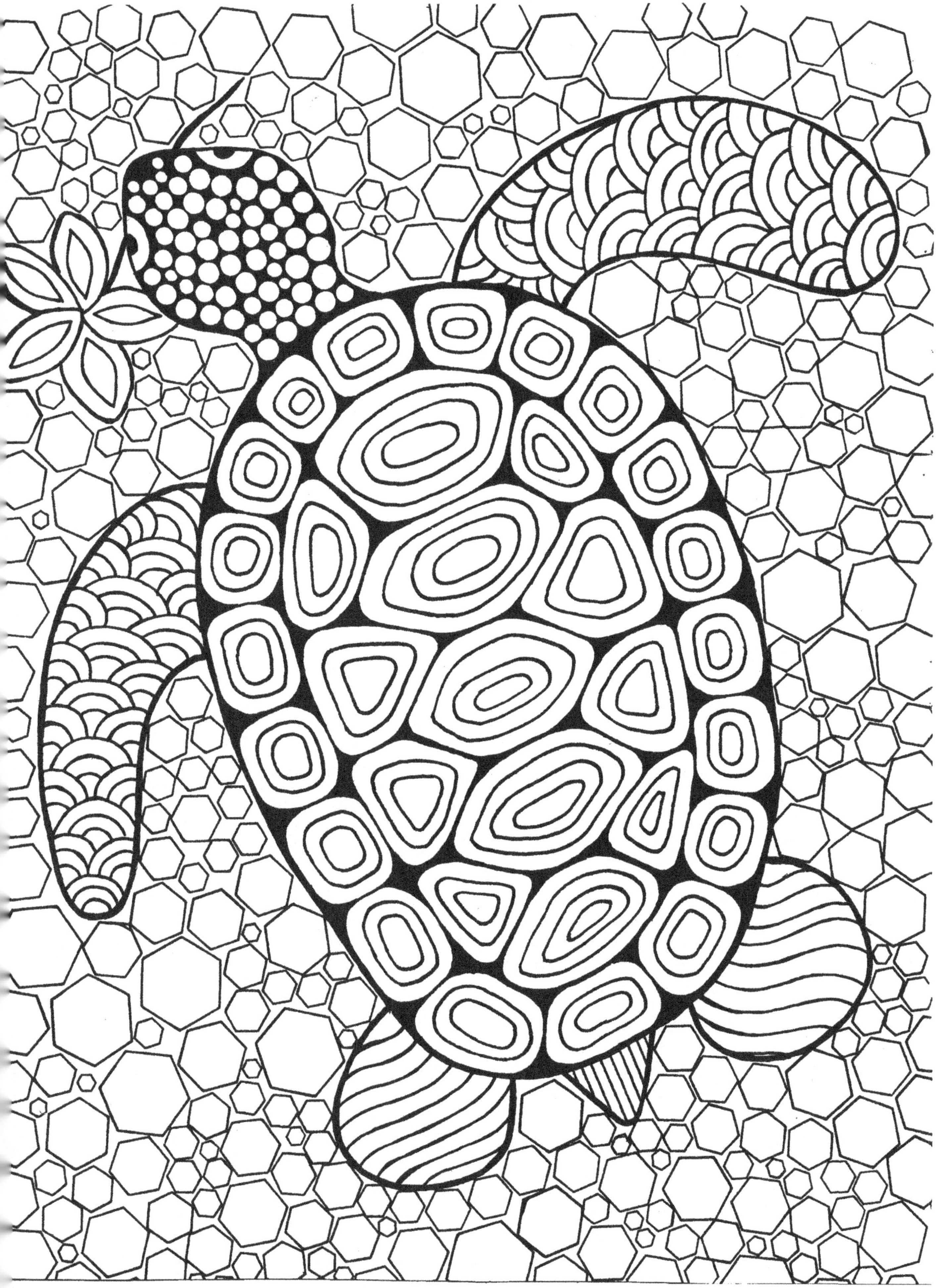

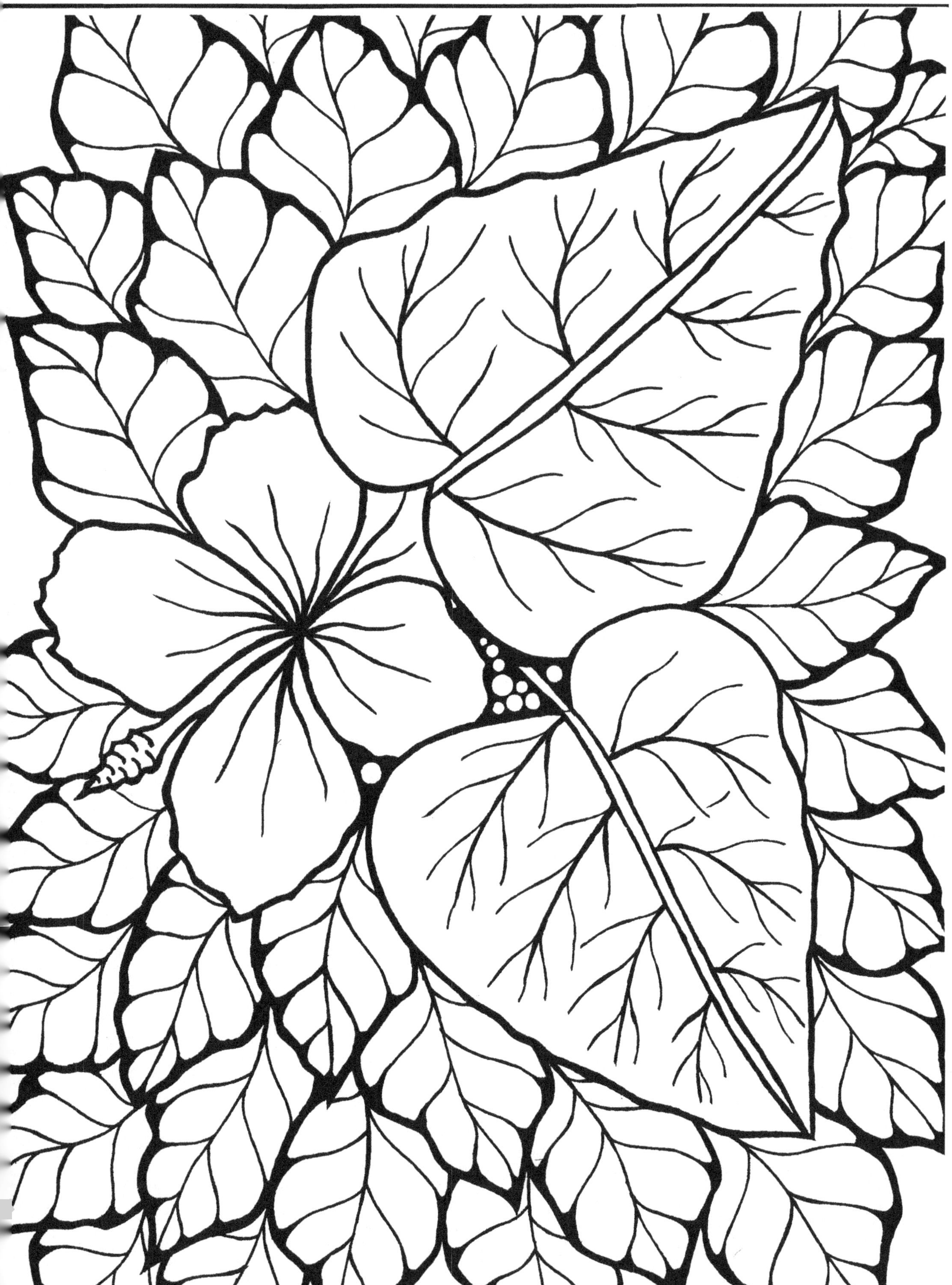

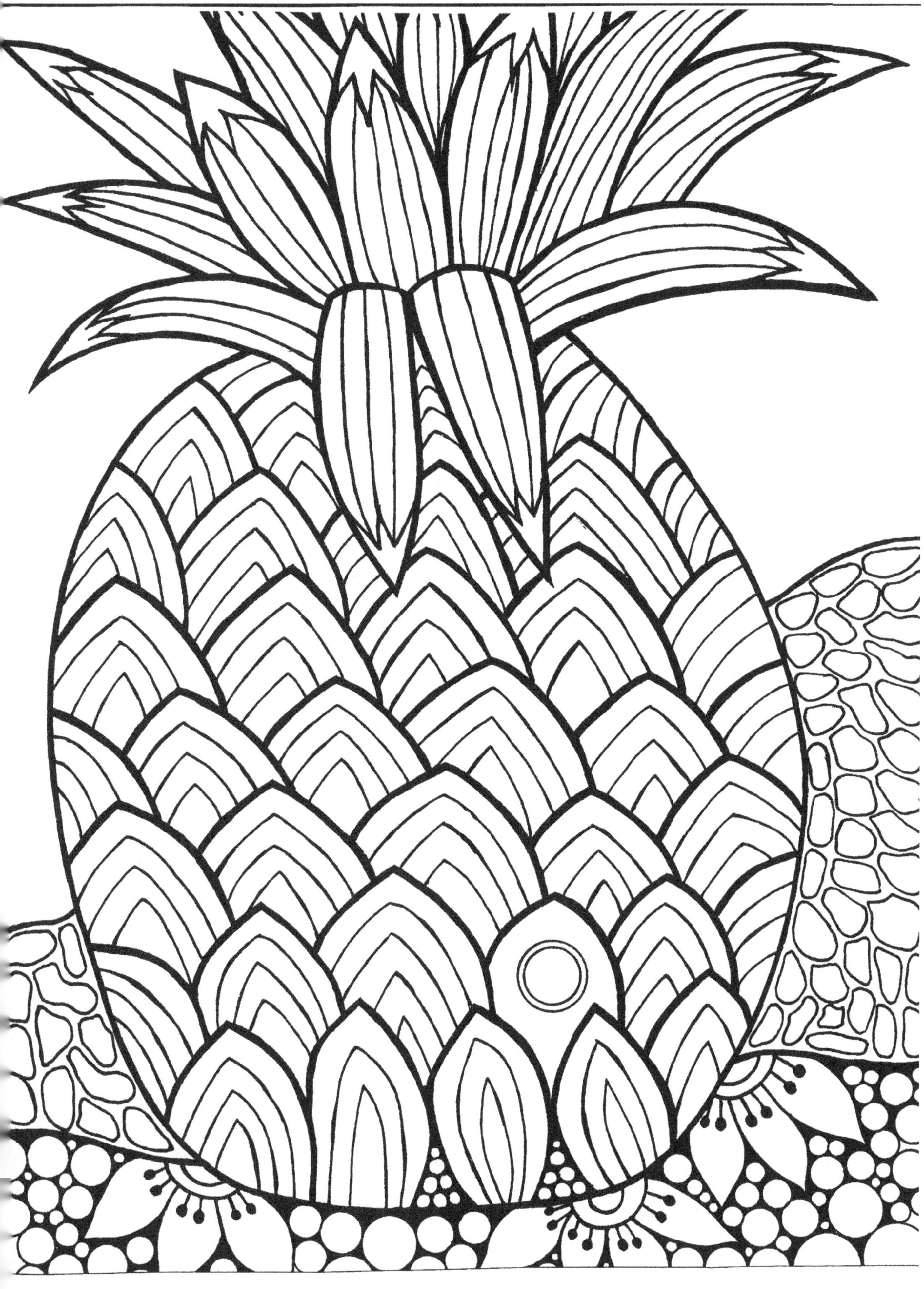

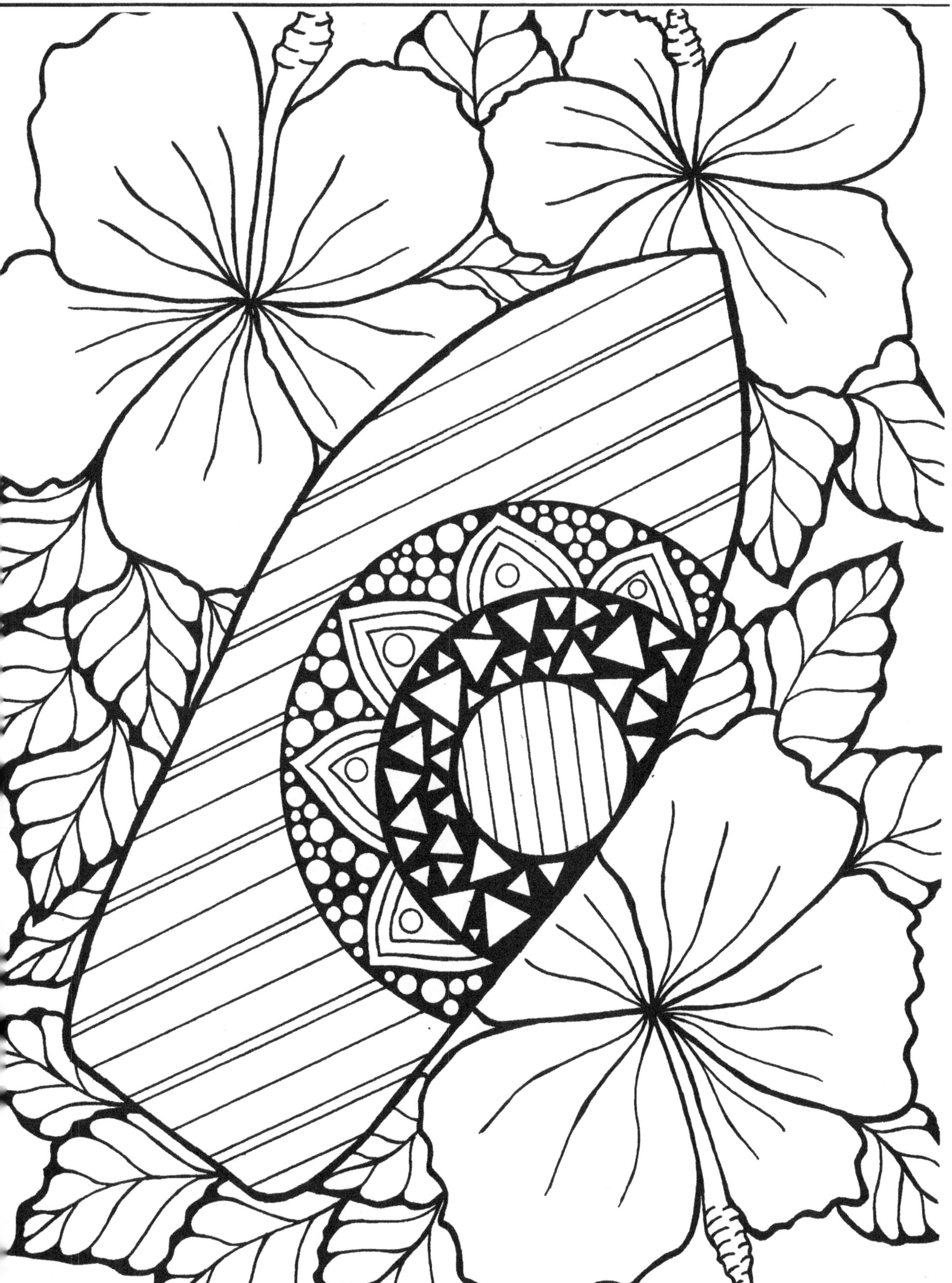

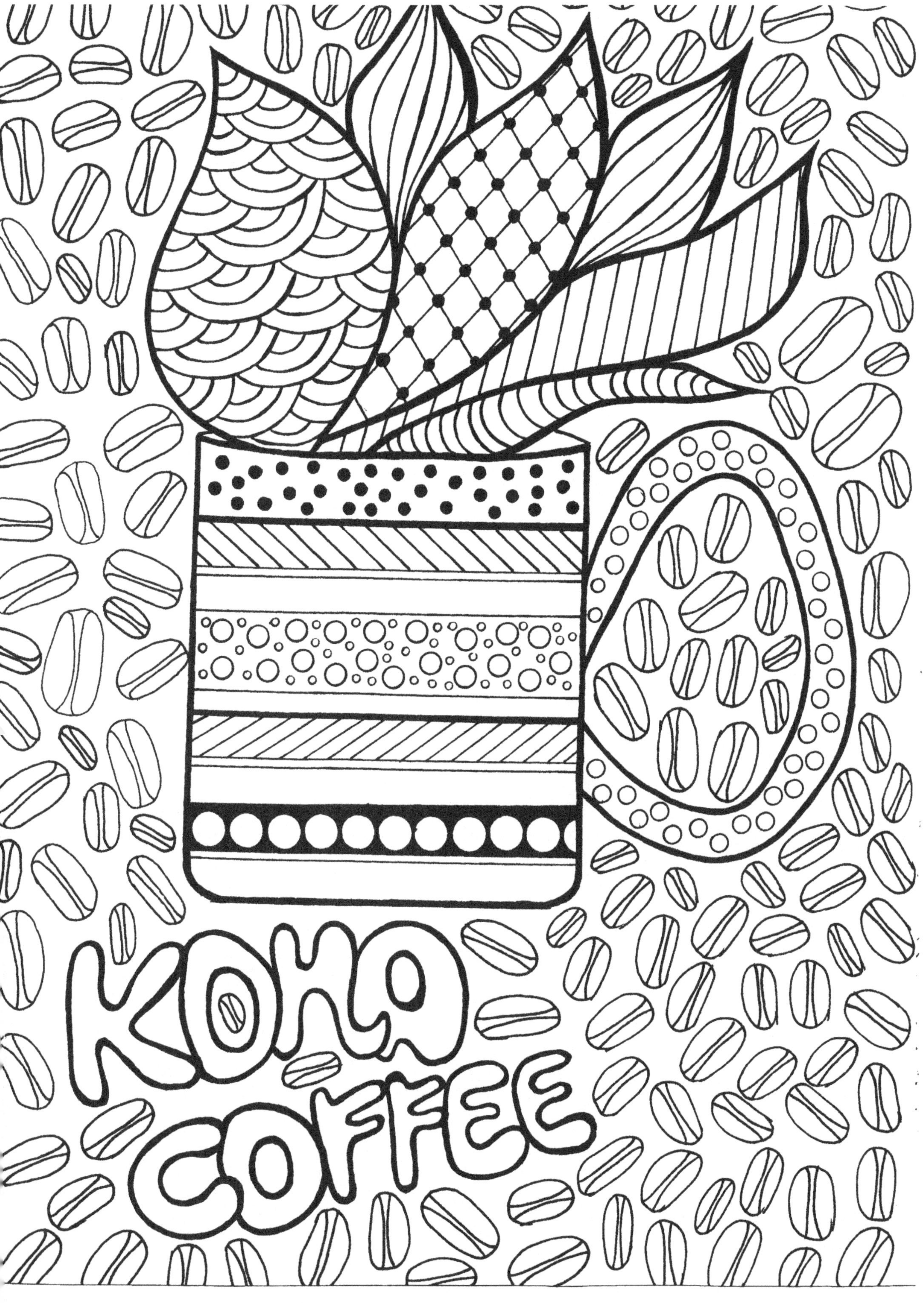
KONA
COFFEE

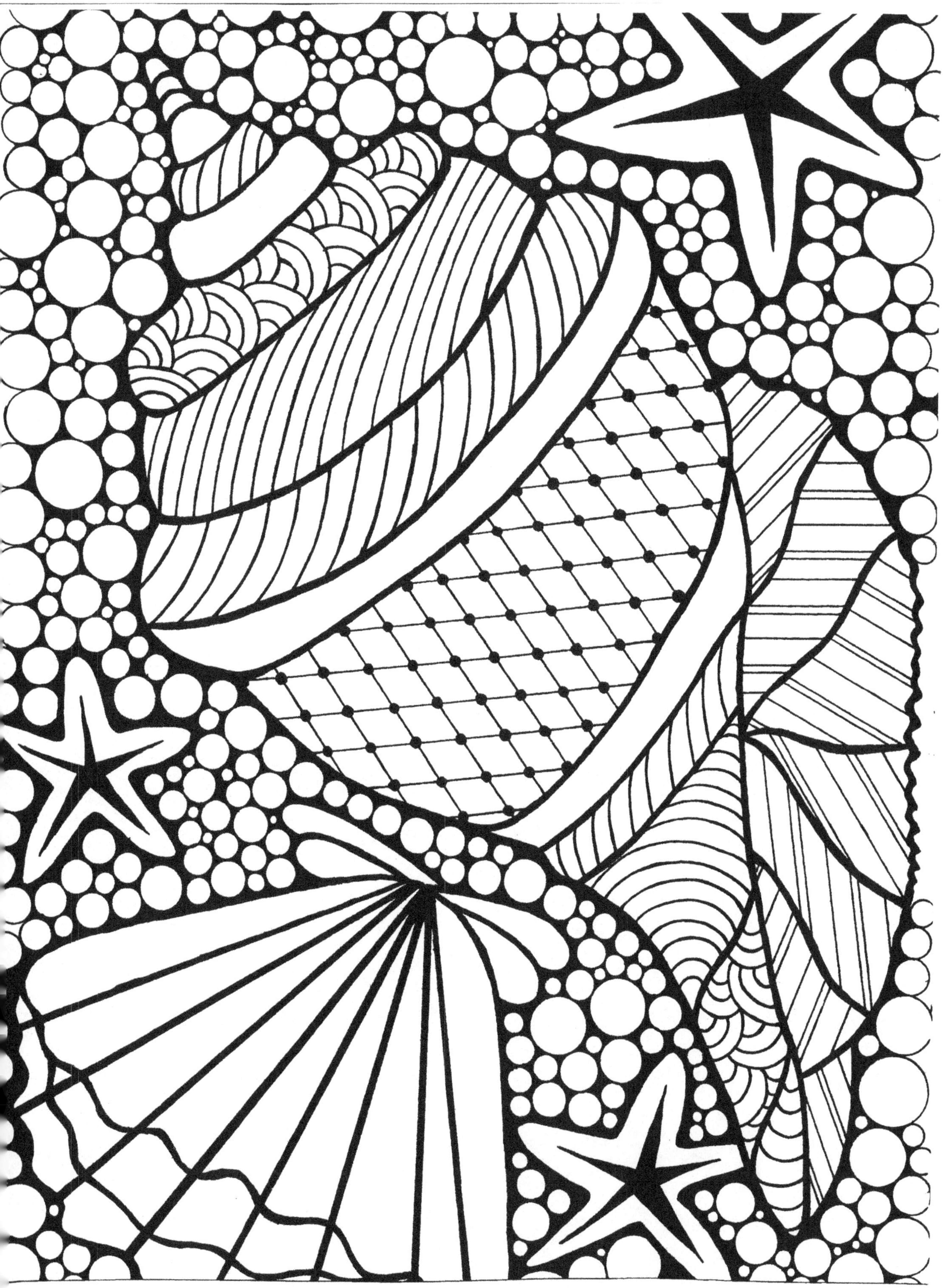

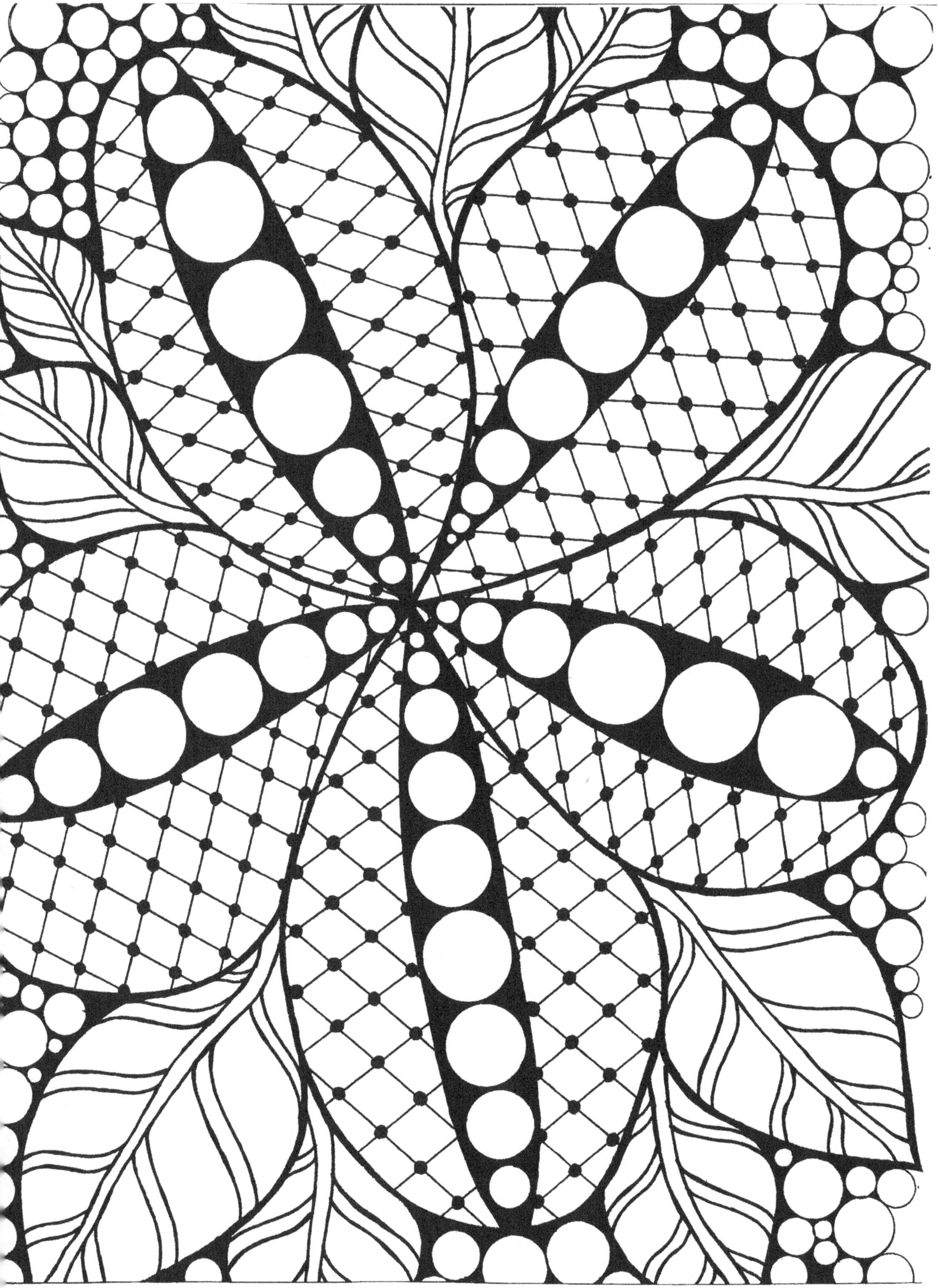

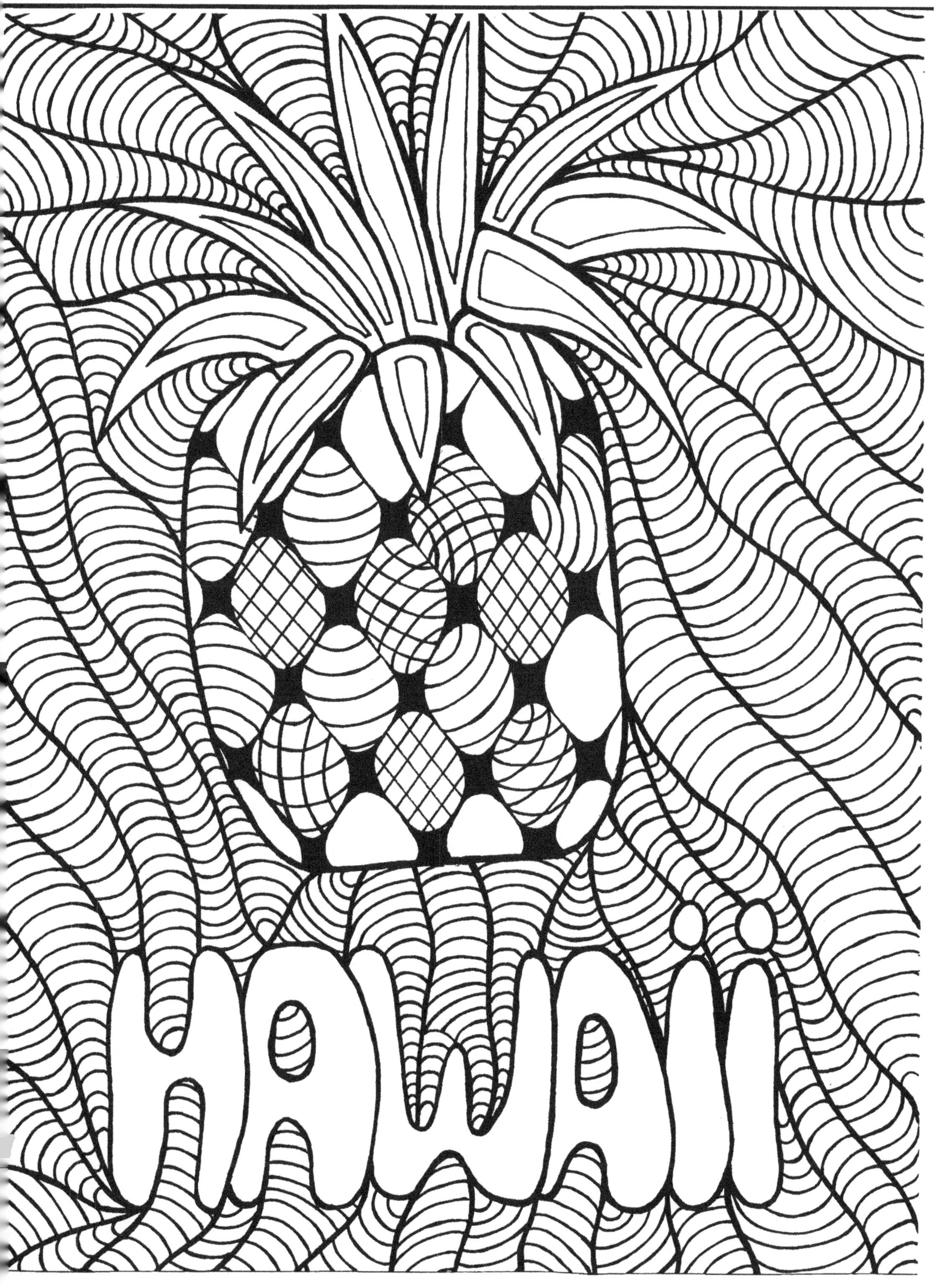
HAWAII

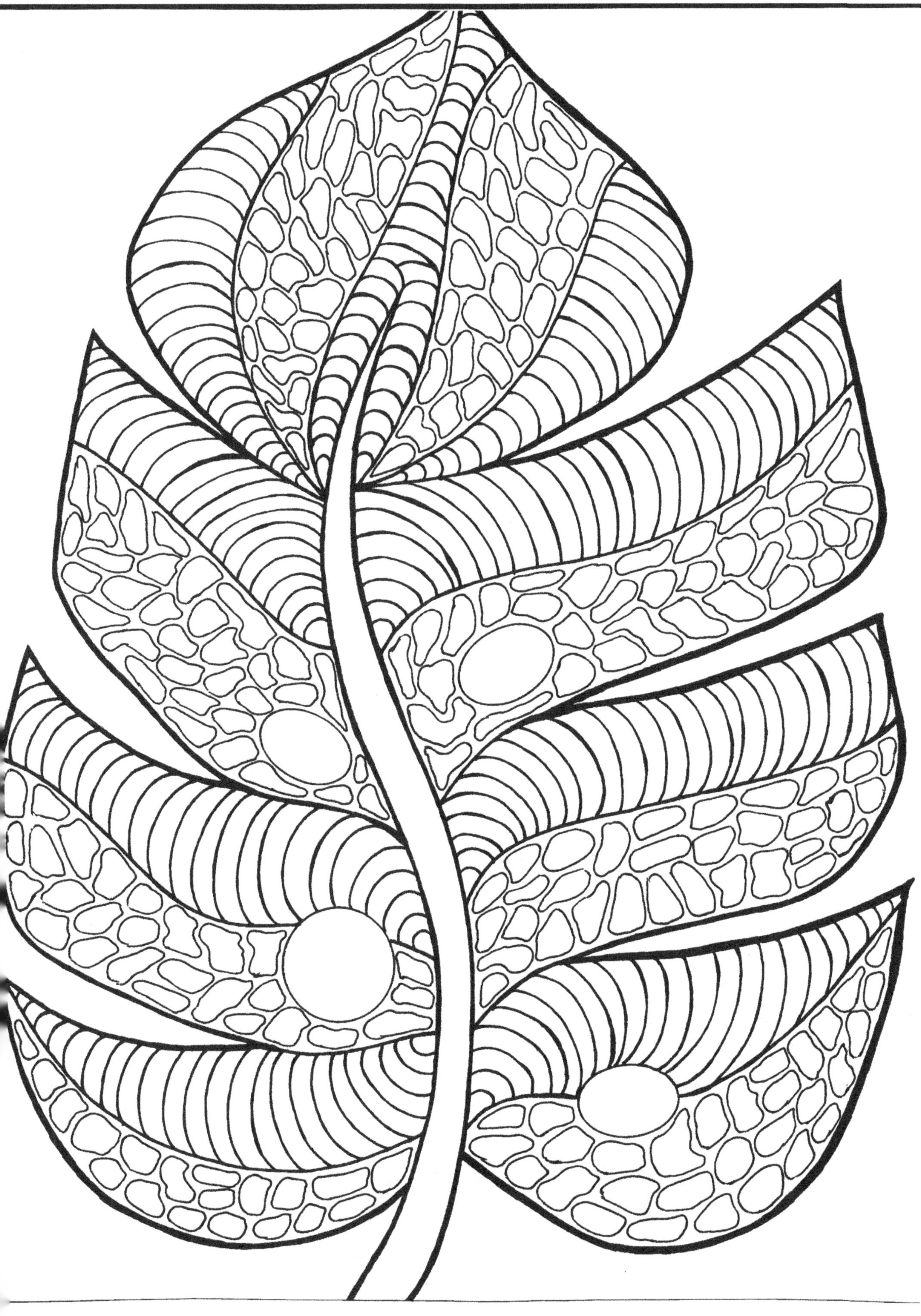

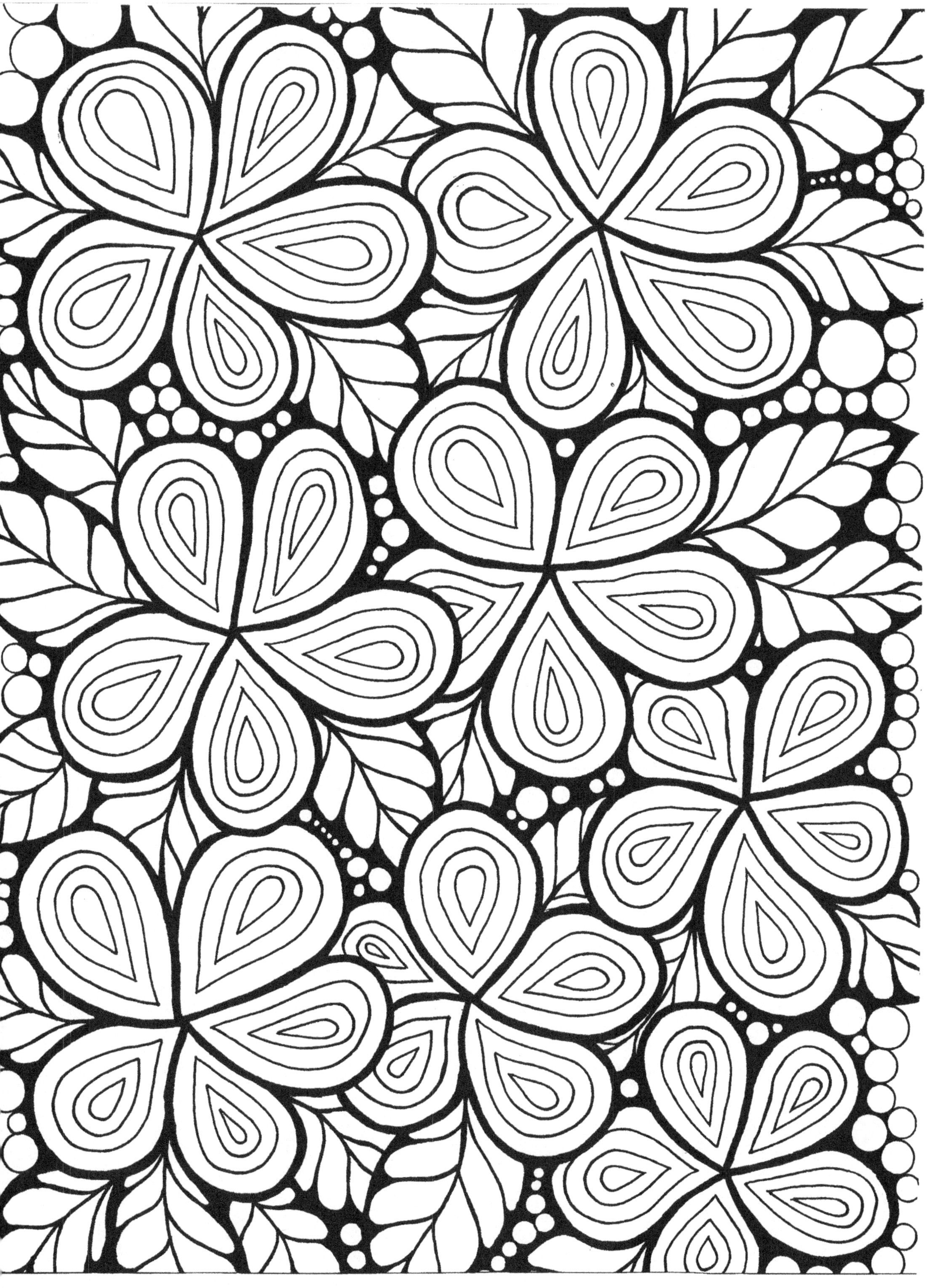

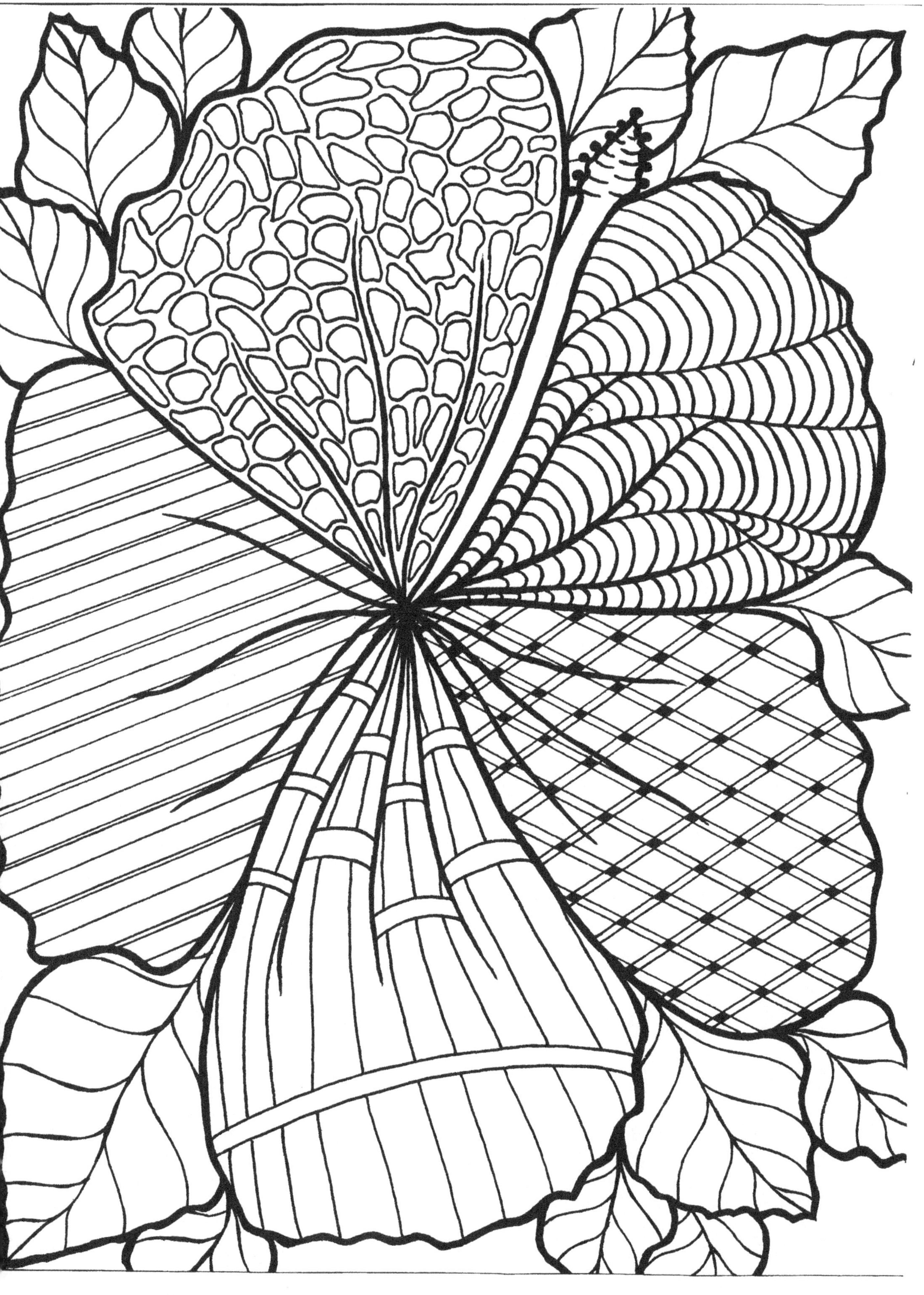

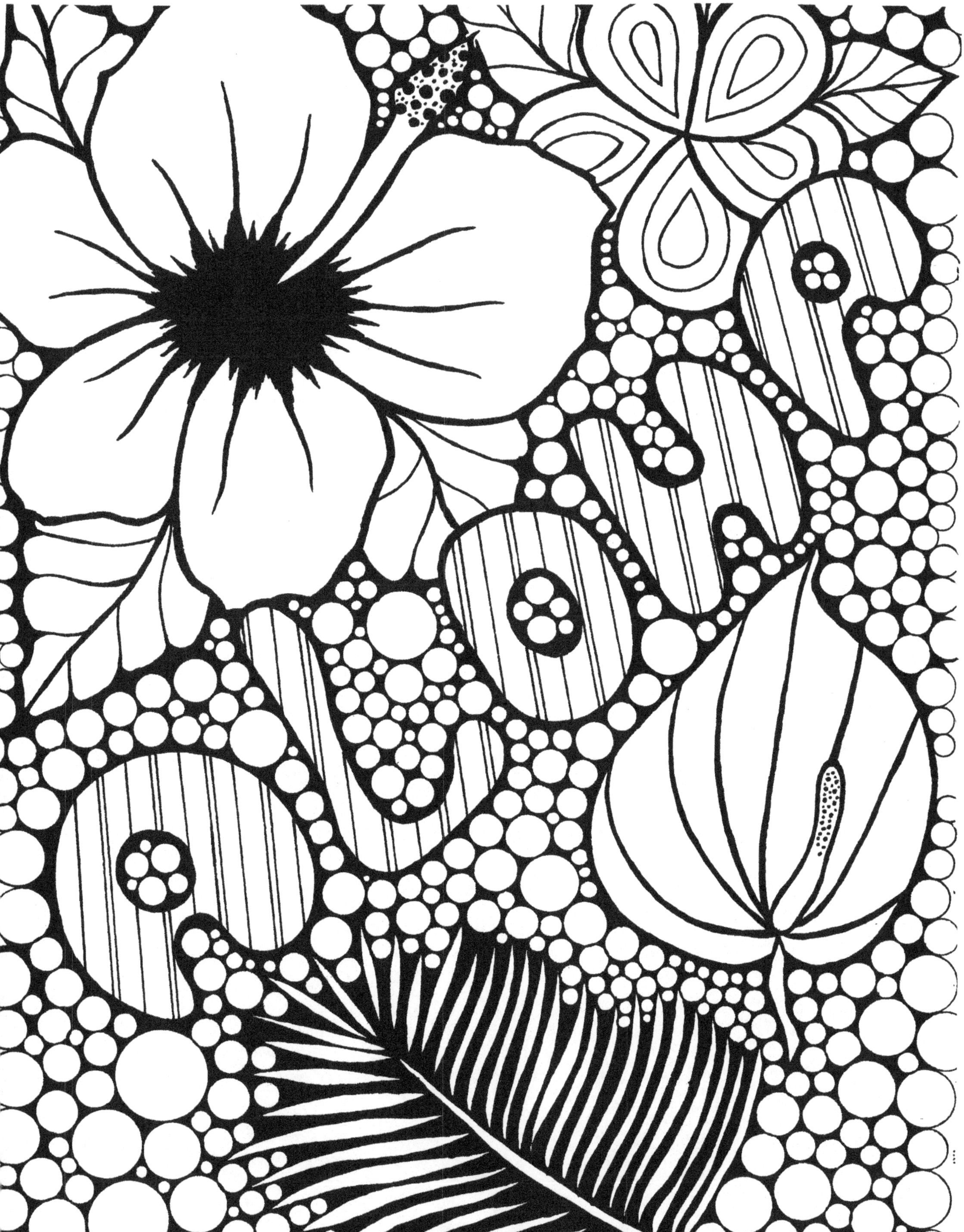

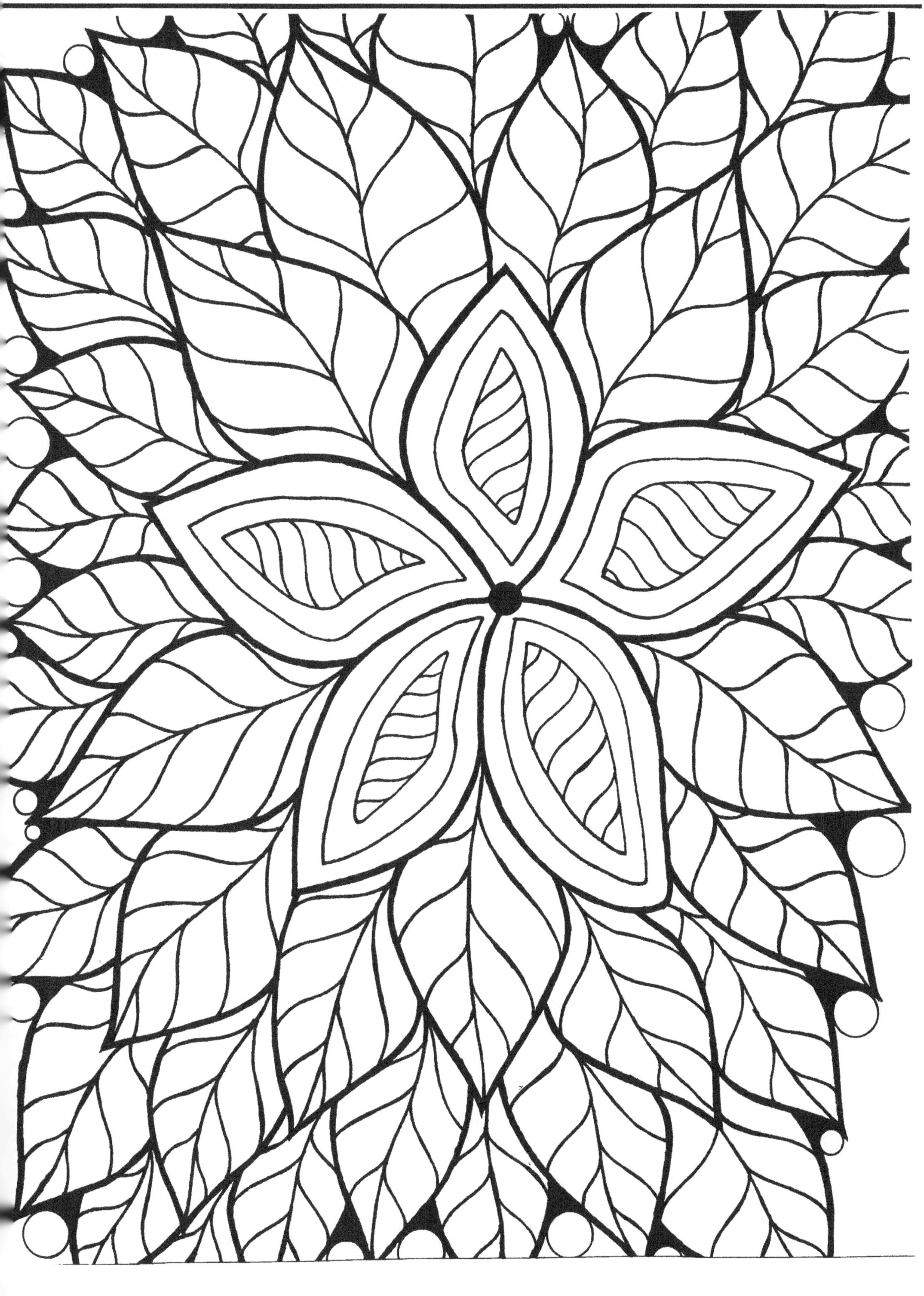

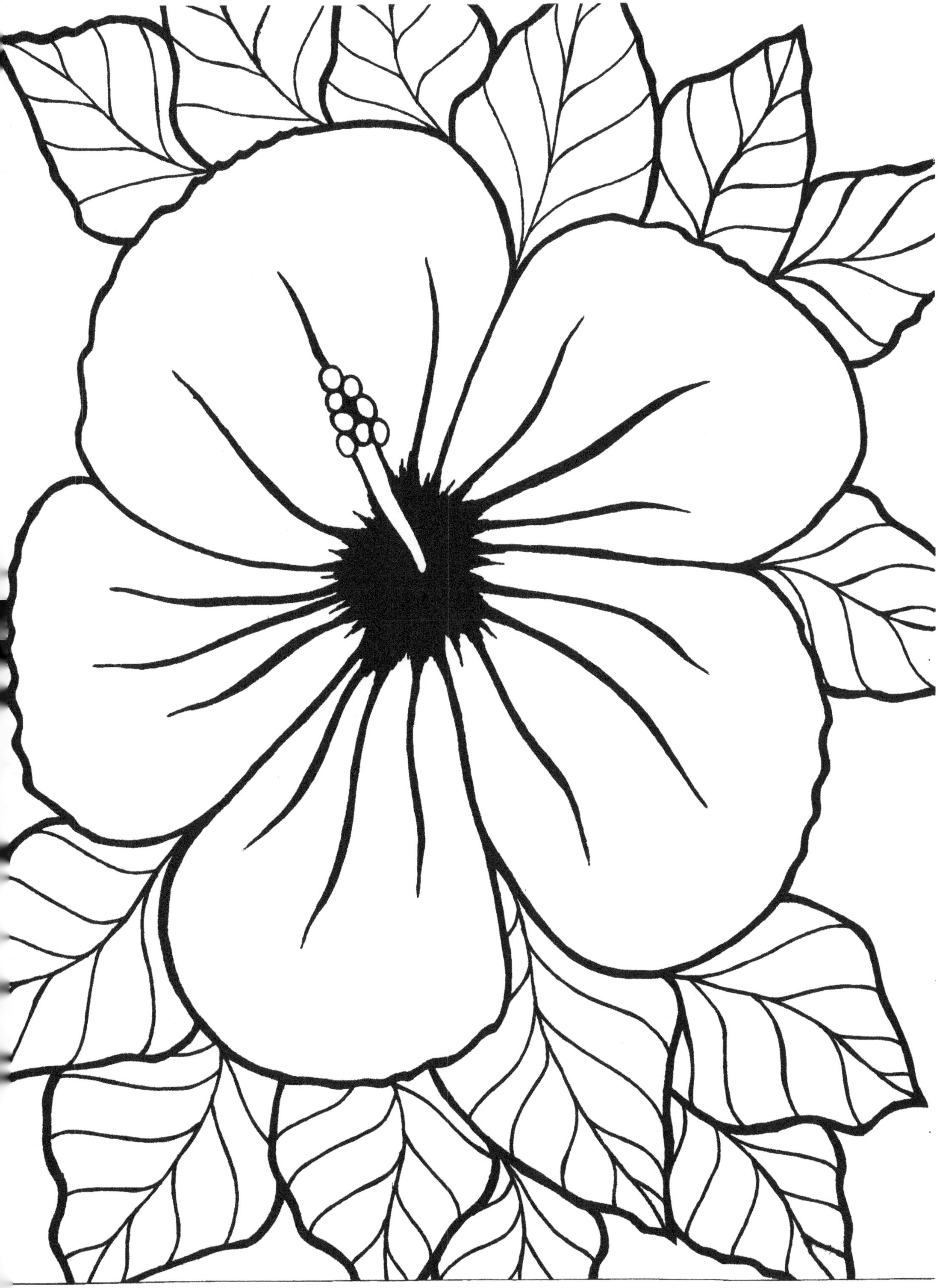

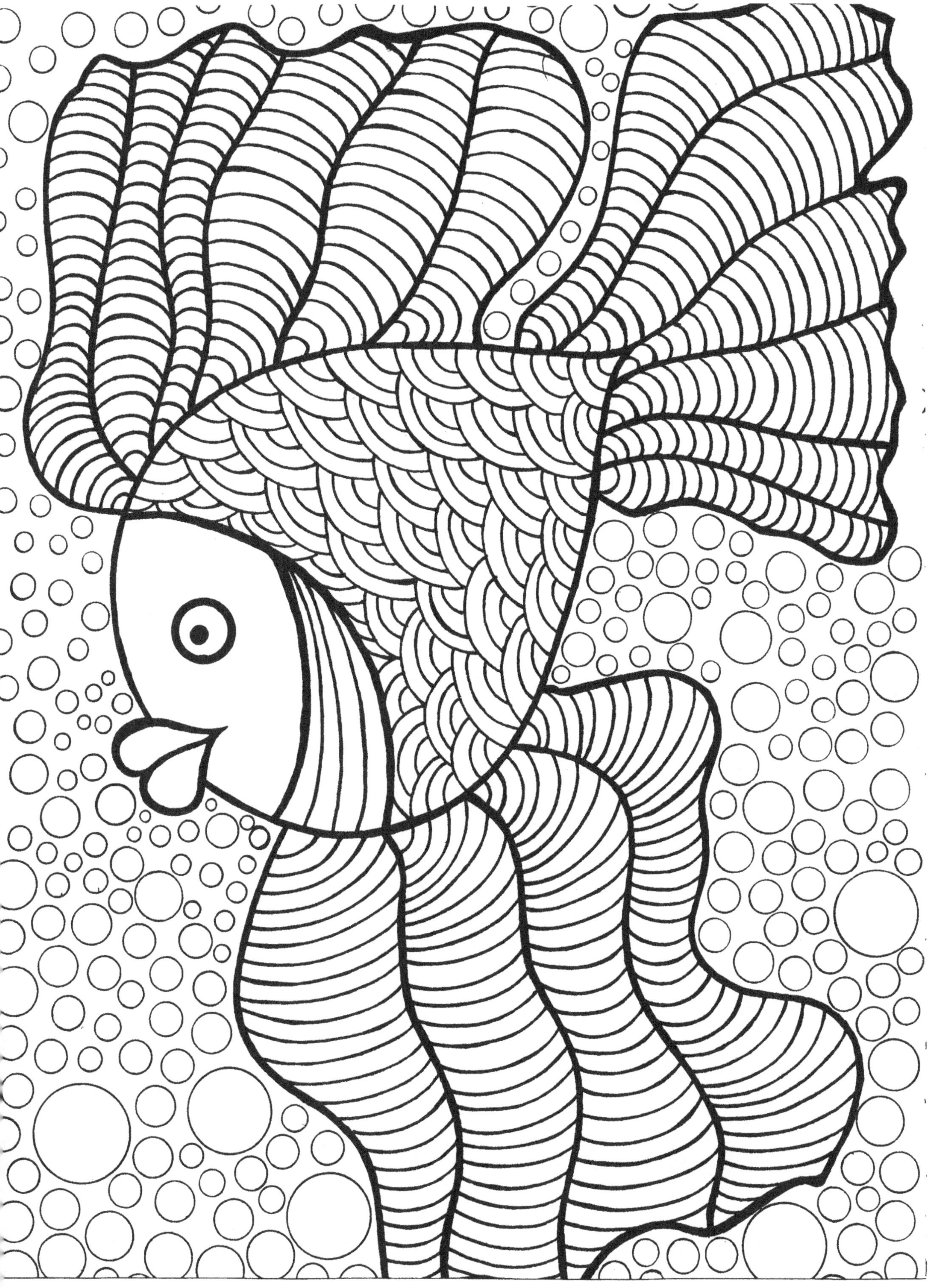

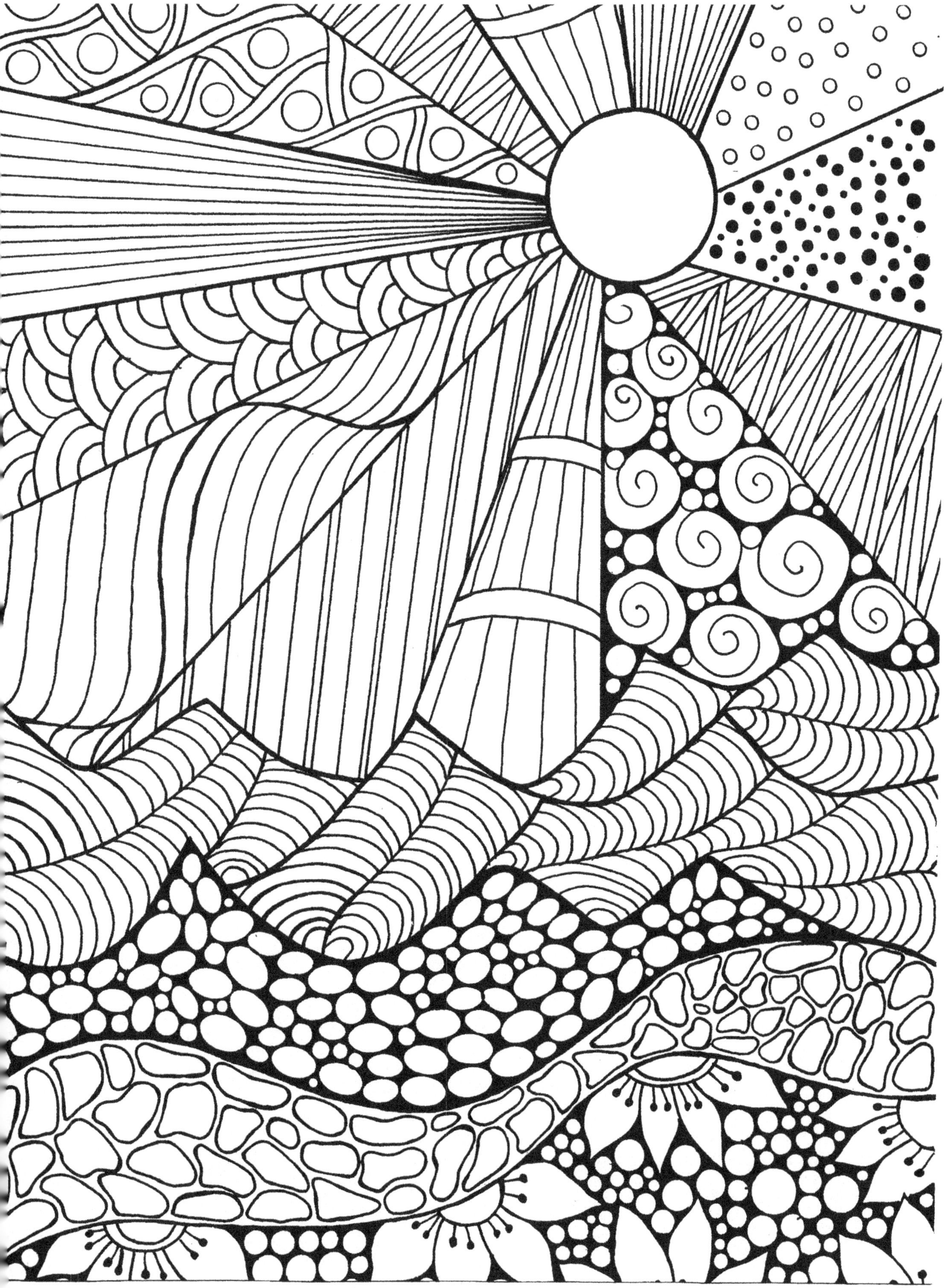

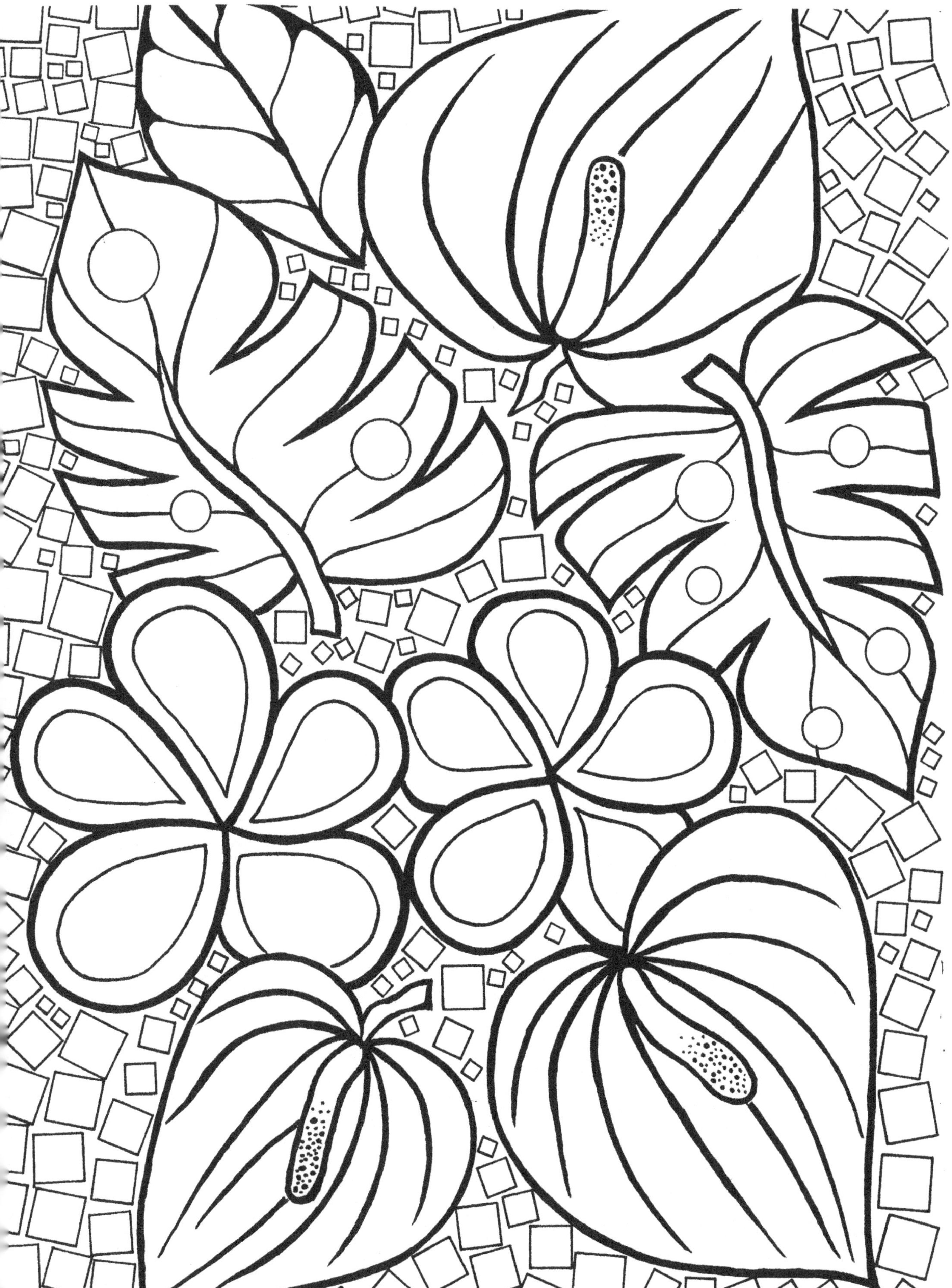

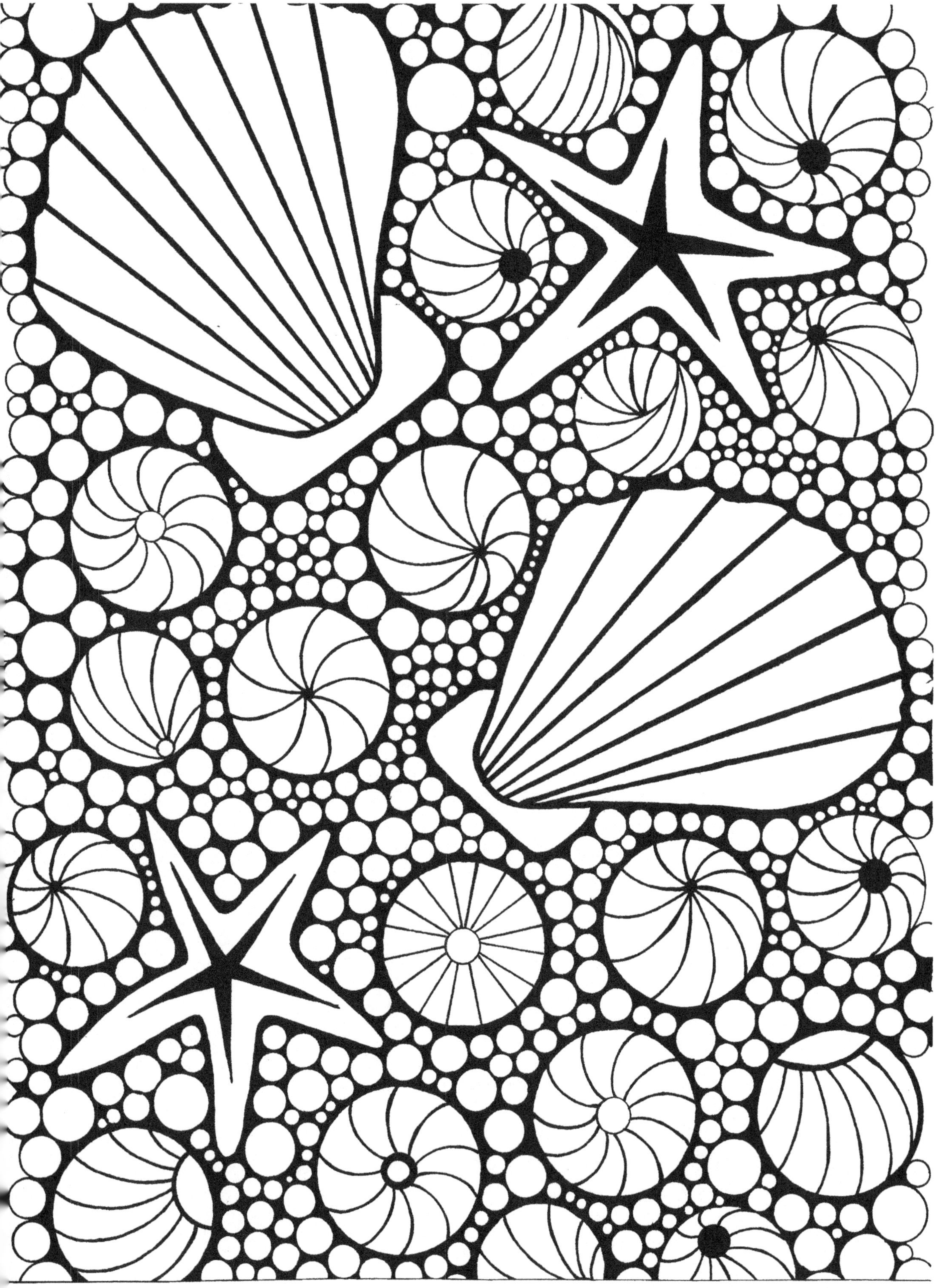

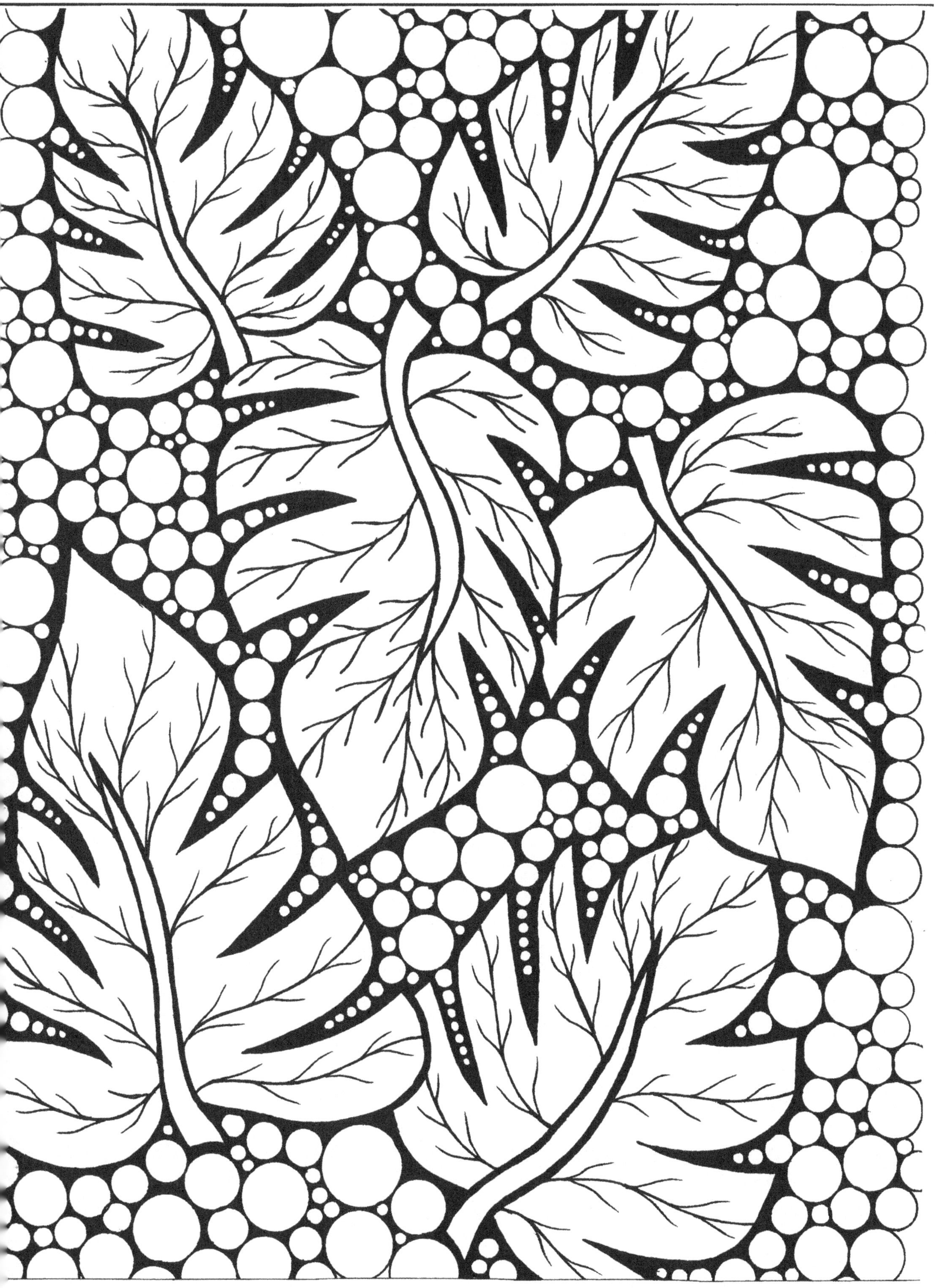

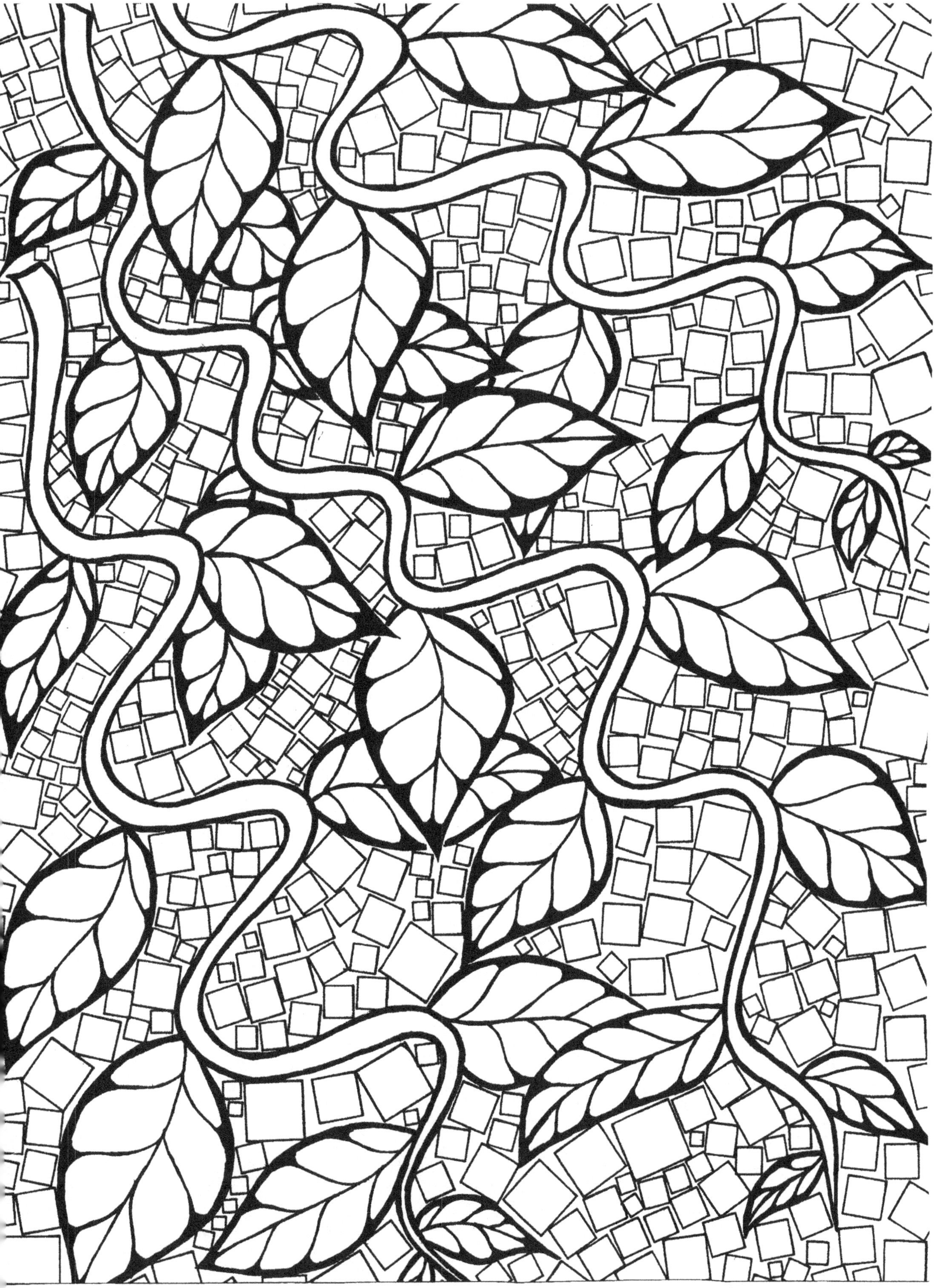

Made in the USA
Coppell, TX
21 June 2023

18360680R00031